In the

MW01235433

*"Deep pain is often
the purest form of love."
Hermann Hesse*

INTRODUCTION

Throughout our lives, we are often accompanied by creatures who, even if they do not speak our language, manage to touch our hearts in ways we could never have imagined.

Pets are more than just companions; they become family members, trusted friends, and for many of us, an inexhaustible source of love and comfort.

Their presence fills our days with joy and their affection supports us in the most difficult moments.

It is a special bond, one of a kind, made of small daily gestures, of glances that speak, of an understanding that goes beyond words.

This book was born from the desire to celebrate that bond, to give voice to those deep emotions that many of us feel, but often struggle to express.

The animals that share our lives don't ask for much: a little food, a warm place and, above all, our love.

In return, they give us everything they have: their unconditional loyalty, their contagious joy, and an affection that knows no reserve.

When we lose them, the void they leave is enormous, and the pain can seem unbearable.

But even in that pain there is beauty, because it is a reflection of how deeply we have been touched by their presence.

The following poems were born from a desire to explore and share this emotional journey.

Every loss is unique, as is every relationship we form with our animal friends.

Some of these poems speak of the sharp pain of loss, others of the sweetness of memories, still others of the healing process and how, over time, we learn to live with the void left by their absence.

I hope these words can offer some comfort to anyone who has known the joy and pain that comes from loving an animal.

I hope they can remind readers that, even in grief, there is room for gratitude and celebration of what has been.

Animals teach us many things: patience, loyalty, the ability to live in the present.

And perhaps the most important lesson is that love never dies.

It lives on in the memories, in the gestures, in the little rituals that remain with us even after they are gone.

This book is dedicated to all those who have loved and lost an animal.

It is a tribute to the deep and indissoluble bond that unites us to them, a bond that transcends time and space, and that continues to live in our hearts, day after day.

"It is the nature of love, once it touches you, that it ties you to that invisible thread that never breaks, not even with death."
Isabel Allende

THE SPECIAL BOND

Beyond Words

In your eyes, a sea of trust,
a silent but so profound language,
where every look was an embrace,
every silence, an entire world.

We didn't need words,
because your heart spoke to mine,
in every shared moment,
there was a universe of emotions.

Even in the darkest moments,
your gaze told me everything,
and in our silence, I found peace,
a bond that went beyond time.

Paws in the Sand

We walked together, step by step,
your paws left footprints,
traces of a simple love,
that time will never be able to erase.

In every grain of sand,
there was a memory of us,
and even if the wind carried them away,
in the heart, they remained intact.

Under the Same Sky

Even when we were far apart,
I knew we were looking at the same sky,
you with your nose to the wind,
me with my heart safe, knowing you were there.

The stars shone for both of us,
guarding our desires,
and every night, under the same sky,
I felt your presence near.

No matter how far apart we were,
our bond remained intact, eternal.

A Heartbeat

Your breathing, a sweet melody,
synchronized with mine,
a symphony of life,
which filled my days with joy.

In every heartbeat, I felt your presence,
a rhythm that accompanied me,
on sunny days and silent nights,
a bond that time could not break.

Even when the world seemed to be falling apart,
your heartbeat was my anchor,
a sound that brought me back to life,
a love that knew no end.

The Joy of Small Gestures

Every wag of your tail, a ray of sunshine,
every bark, an extra laugh,
every leap of joy, an
invitation to live in the present moment.

In your little gestures, I found happiness,
a simplicity that filled my heart,
reminding me that life is made of moments,
and that every moment with you was precious.

Life Companions

You have been my silent confidant,
my companion on bright and dark days,
always there, no questions asked,
only with love to give.

You saw my every tear,
heard my every sigh,
and without saying a word,
you knew how to console me like no one else.

Whenever the world
became too big,
it was you who brought me back to reality,
with your reassuring presence,
your unconditional love.

We shared moments of pure joy,
and moments of deep sadness,
but every moment,
you were there, my faithful companion,
my refuge, my friend,
my endless love.

The Warmth of Your Presence

In your every gesture, an unconditional affection,
in your every caress, a world of comfort,
you were the warmth on a cold day,
the refuge in the storms of life.

When all seemed lost,
your presence brought me back to serenity,
reminding me that, as long as you were there,
there was nothing to fear.

Even in the most difficult moments,
your love was my strength,
a warmth that enveloped me,
a love that protected me.

A Friendship Without Words

We didn't need words,
your closeness said it all,
a bond that went beyond time,
beyond space, beyond the possible.

Every look of yours, a message,
every gesture of yours, a sign of affection,
that knew no barriers,
and that spoke directly to the heart.

It was a friendship made of silences,
of deep and indestructible complicity.

Simply Together

It didn't matter what we did,
as long as we were together,
because in every moment we shared,
there was all the meaning in the world.

Whether it was a leisurely stroll
or a sunny afternoon,
your presence made
every moment special,
because we were simply together.

A Safe Haven

In the midst of the chaos of life,
you were my safe haven,
a place where I could be myself,
knowing that you would be there, always.

When the world hurt me,
I found comfort in your embrace,
a love that asked for nothing,
just to be, to exist together.

Every time life hit me,
it was you who lifted me up,
with your sweetness,
with your silent but powerful presence.

You offered me a refuge,
a place of peace and serenity,
where I could find the strength to move forward,
knowing that, with you by my side,
there was no obstacle we couldn't overcome.

Simple Love

There was no complexity in our bond,
just pure and simple love,
like a cloudless sky,
like a field of flowers in spring.

Your love was my anchor,
my safe harbor,
an affection that knew no conditions,
that wrapped me like a cloak.

It was a love made of small gestures,
glances and shared silences.

The Rhythm of Life

Living next to you, I learned
the rhythm of nature,
the time marked by your steps,
your games and your breaks,
a time that has become ours.

We danced together in the rhythm of life,
following the cycles of nature,
from bright dawns to serene starry nights,
a rhythm that united us in an eternal bond.

Even when the days
seemed to go by endlessly,
I knew that our rhythm was unique,
a beat that kept us united,
in the heart of life.

The Magic of Ordinary Days

Every day with you was special,
even the ordinary ones,
because you knew how to transform
routine into magic,
with a simple gesture, a whisper, a whimper.

There was no need for big events,
your presence was enough,
because in every ordinary day,
there was a spark of happiness.

Together we have created a daily magic,
which will continue to shine in my heart.

A Bond That Goes Beyond

Even when you were not by my side,
I felt your affection enveloping me,
a bond that went beyond distance,
beyond the visible, beyond time.

Your love accompanied me everywhere,
an invisible thread that tied us together,
and that not even distance
could break.

Light in the Dark Days

In the darkest days, you were my light,
the smile that brought me back to life,
the presence that reminded me
that I was never alone.

Even when all seemed lost,
your light shone for me,
a beacon to guide me through the storms,
a love that knew no darkness.

In every caress of yours, I found hope,
in every look of yours, I found strength,
and I knew that, with you by my side,
I could face anything.

A Love Without Pretensions

You never asked for anything in return,
just my company,
and in return you gave me everything,
an unpretentious, infinite love.

Your affection was pure and sincere,
a source of joy every day,
a gift I will never stop appreciating,
a love I will always carry with me.

The Silence That Speaks

With you, I learned the value of silence,
a silence that spoke of complicity,
of deep understanding,
of a bond that did not need words.

In that silence, there was everything,
our friendship, our love,
a voiceless dialogue
that united us more than a thousand words.

It was in silence that we found peace,
a silence that spoke straight to the heart.

A Love That Heals

Every time life hurt me,
you were there to heal me,
with your sweet and reassuring presence,
with your love that healed every wound.

Your caresses were balm,
your eyes were refuge,
and in the most difficult moments,
it was you who gave me the strength to continue.

You have cared not only for my body,
but also for my soul,
and for that,
I will be forever grateful to you,
because your love has made me a better person.

The Invisible Embrace

Even when I couldn't touch you,
I felt your invisible embrace,
a warmth that enveloped me,
a love that supported me.

It was a hug that went beyond physicality,
a bond that knew no boundaries,
and that continued to give me strength,
even in moments of solitude.

Always by My Side

In every step I take,
in every road I walk,
I know that you are still by my side,
because a bond like ours knows no end.

Even though I can no longer see you,
I feel you close,
like a faithful shadow,
accompanying me everywhere.

You are the strength
that pushes me forward,
the light that guides me in dark times,
and even when the road is difficult,
I know you are there, walking with me.

Our bond is made of memories,
love and shared moments,
a bond that never breaks,
not even with time,
because the love that united us
will live on forever, in every step,
in every breath, always by my side,
always with me.

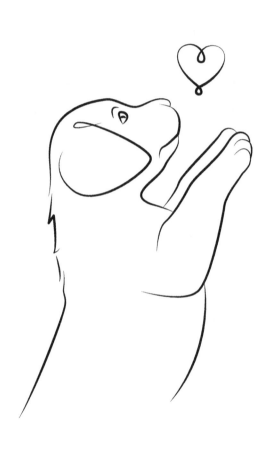

*"I didn't know how deeply an
animal could enter my life
until I had to let it go."*
Anonymous

THE PAIN OF LOSS

Tears Without Voice

The tears fall silently,
without voice, without sound,
a pain that envelops me,
an emptiness that finds no peace.

Every corner of the house
speaks to me of you,
and in this deafening silence,
I miss you more than ever.

A Void in the Heart

You left a void in my heart,
an absence that weighs like a boulder,
every beat is a memory of you,
every breath, a whisper of your name.

Your presence was a constant,
a love that knew no end,
and now, without you,
the world seems colder,
darker, more distant.

I miss you in every little gesture,
in every quiet moment,
and this emptiness in my heart
reminds me how important you were.

The Last Look

Your last look broke me,
a goodbye I wasn't ready to give,
the pain wraps me like a cloak,
leaving only shadows of what you were.

I relive that moment a thousand times,
seeking comfort in memories,
but each time, your gaze pierces me,
a pain that does not seem to go away.

Without You

Without you, the house is empty,
every room resonates with your silence,
a distant echo of your footsteps,
which I can no longer hear.

Every corner speaks to me of you,
but it is a dialogue made of absences,
of spaces that are not filled,
of a love that finds no peace.

Without you, everything is different,
and the world seems less alive, less mine.

A Painful Goodbye

I said goodbye to you with a broken heart,
knowing that nothing would ever be the same,
the pain hit me suddenly,
a blow that I still can't bear.

Every memory of you is a scalpel,
sinking into my chest,
leaving deep scars,
indelible signs of a lost love.

I look for you in my dreams,
hoping to find you again,
but even in dreams, the farewell is bitter,
and the pain does not subside,
does not calm down.

The Day You Went

I remember the day you went,
the sky seemed to cry with me,
every drop of rain, a tear,
every thunder, a cry of pain.

The world stopped for a moment,
as you took flight,
leaving behind only silence,
a void I can't fill.

I walk the places you loved,
hoping to find you there again,
but all I find are shadows,
and an absence that consumes me.

The day you went away,
I lost a part of me,
a piece of my heart,
that will never come back.

And now, even as time passes,
the pain remains alive,
a memory of that day,
when everything changed forever.

Without Your Breath

The house is silent without your breathing,
a void filling every room,
the nights are longer,
and the days seem colorless.

I try to fill this silence,
but nothing can replace your presence,
and every breath I take
reminds me that you are no longer here.

The Pain of Loneliness

Every morning I wake up,
hoping to find you still here,
but loneliness greets me,
and pain pierces my heart.

You were my constant, my strength,
and now, without you,
I feel lost, at a loss,
like a ship without a course.

Loneliness is a burden I carry,
a pain that never eases.

Shadows of Pain

Everywhere I look, I see shadows of pain,
memories of you that suddenly surface,
like ghosts of a happy past,
that now torment me relentlessly.

Every corner, every object,
carries your presence,
a reminder of what we were,
of what will never return.

The shadows follow me everywhere,
they envelop me in their icy embrace,
and I can't escape
this pain that won't let me go.

The Silence of the Morning

Morning comes, but without you,
the silence is deeper, sharper,
every ray of sunshine seems cold,
and the house is immersed in
a shadow of sadness.

You are no longer there to wake me up gently,
with your reassuring presence,
and every morning without you,
is a reminder of what I have lost.

The silence of the morning weighs on me,
a pain I can't ignore.

A Farewell Without Words

There were no words,
just a silent goodbye,
a moment I lived in apnea,
without knowing how to move on.

You left me without saying goodbye,
and now I find myself lost in grief,
trying to fill the void
with memories that are never enough.

Tears in the Wind

I cried tears into the wind,
hoping your spirit would catch them,
that you would feel my pain,
that you would know how much I miss you.

The wind took away my tears,
scattered them into the sky,
but the pain remained,
a wound that never heals.

Every day, I look to the sky,
searching for a sign of you,
but all I find
is the cold embrace of the wind.

The tears continue to fall,
like rain on a desolate field,
and the wind carries them away,
but not my pain.

The Weight of Absence

Every day I wake up with the weight of
your absence,
a burden that I carry in my heart,
every step is more difficult,
every breath is a memory of you.

Your absence is like a shadow,
that follows me wherever I go,
I can't escape this pain, that
grips me, that suffocates me.

I've tried to fill the void you left,
but nothing can replace your presence,
and every attempt to move on
seems futile, pointless, without you.

The world continues to turn,
but I remain still,
stuck in this pain,
which holds me prisoner.

And even as time passes,
your absence weighs like a boulder,
a weight I can't lift,
a pain I can't let go.

Broken Memories

Memories of you are broken,
fragments that surface in my mind,
like pieces of an unfinished puzzle,
leaving me with a sense of emptiness.

Every memory is a sharp blade,
cutting my heart without mercy,
and as I try to reconstruct what we were,
I realize that nothing will ever be the same again.

Broken memories haunt me,
a pain that finds no peace.

A Broken Dream

I had dreamed of a future with you,
but that dream was shattered,
leaving me with only the fragments,
of a love that will never live.

Now I find myself wandering,
between what has been and what will not be,
trying to pick up the pieces
of a dream that will never come true.

The Day After

The day after you left,
the world seemed different,
everything had lost color,
every sound was muffled, distant.

I tried to find comfort,
but every attempt was in vain,
because without you,
nothing made sense anymore.

The next day, I realized
that my world had changed forever.

The Absence That Screams

Your absence cries out in the silence,
a silent scream that tears my soul apart,
every moment without you
is a wound that cannot heal.

I search for your face in memories,
but all I find
is a faded shadow,
an echo of what you were.

Absence has become my companion,
a pain that accompanies me every day,
and every night, when the silence falls,
your absence cries out even louder.

An Endless Pain

The pain of your loss is never-ending,
it is a wave that overwhelms me,
drags me into the depths of memory,
where everything is clouded by your absence.

Every moment with you was precious,
every day a blessing,
and now that you are gone,
I feel lost, bewildered, incomplete.

Pain has become a part of me,
a silent companion that never leaves me,
and even in moments of apparent serenity,
I feel its weight, its cold embrace.

There is no consolation that can soothe
this wound, no words that
can fill the void,
and while the world continues to spin,
I remain here, trapped in pain.

But even in this pain, I find a reflection
of our love, a love that was pure,
sincere, and that continues to live in me,
even if now it is shrouded in sadness.

Shadows of Absence

I walk among shadows of absence,
every step brings me back to you,
but your smile is no longer there,
only an emptiness that envelops me.

Shadows follow me everywhere,
memories of what was,
and in every shadow I find your reflection,
a love that never fades.

A Lost Love

I lost a love that will never return,
a bond that cannot be broken,
but now lives only in memories,
a pain that I carry in my heart.

Every day without you is a torment,
a reminder of what I've lost,
and as I try to move on,
I realize that nothing will ever be the same.

Your love was everything to me,
and without you, I feel lost.

"When an animal you love becomes a memory, that memory becomes a treasure."
Anonymous

THE MEMORY

In the Silence of Time

In the silence of time,
your memory still lives,
a distant, sweet and constant echo
that accompanies me every day.

Even if you are no longer here,
your presence remains alive,
in the folds of my heart,
in every breath, in every thought.

Shadows of Memory

Shadows of memory dance around me,
memories of you surfacing,
like gentle ghosts,
bringing the past back to light.

Every laugh, every game,
is engraved in my mind,
every caress, every look,
remains imprinted in my heart.

Even as time passes,
shadows do not vanish,
they are the trace of our bond,
the indelible sign of our love.

A Hidden Smile

In the folds of time,
I find a hidden smile,
a memory of you that warms my heart,
even on the coldest days.

That smile is a refuge,
a safe harbor in the storm,
a memory that never fades,
and that makes me feel less alone.

The Traces of Your Passage

The traces of your passage
are still visible in my heart,
every gesture, every look,
has left an indelible mark.

I remember your light steps,
your way of making every day special,
and even if you are no longer here,
the traces of your love remain.

Every corner of my life
carries a sign of you.

An Echo of Tenderness

Your memory is an echo of tenderness,
which resonates sweetly in my heart,
every day, every night,
it accompanies me like a sweet melody.

Even as time passes,
the echo does not fade away,
it continues to play,
reminding me of the beauty of our bond.

Every time I close my eyes,
I feel your presence,
an echo that comforts me,
that envelops me in a silent embrace.

Between the Pages of the Heart

Between the pages of my heart,
memories of you are written,
each page tells a story,
each story is a fragment of us.

I remember the sunny days, t
he runs in the fields,
the quiet moments
spent together, in silence.

Every page is filled with your love,
every word is a whisper of the past,
a memory that will never fade,
that will remain with me forever.

Even when the book of life closes,
the pages of the heart will remain open,
to tell our story,
a love that has transcended time.

And every time I browse those pages,
I feel your presence close by,
a memory that lives,
that still breathes.

A Ray of Sunshine

Your memory is a ray of sunshine,
which lights up my darkest days,
even when the sky is overcast,
your love still shines.

Every morning, when the sun rises,
I see your smile reflected in the rays,
and the warmth of your memory
warms my heart.

A Voice in the Wind

In the wind I hear your voice,
a whisper that speaks to me softly,
tells me of days gone by,
of moments that will never fade.

Even though I can no longer touch you,
your voice rings clear,
guiding me, comforting me,
in every step I take.

The wind carries your memory,
 a song that never fades.

A Scent of Memories

There is a scent in the air,
a sweet and familiar aroma,
that brings me back to you,
to the days we shared.

Every time I hear it,
I close my eyes and I see you again,
alive, present, next to me,
as if you had never left.

The scent of memories is a balm
that soothes the wounds of the heart,
envelops me in an invisible embrace,
a bond that never breaks.

Footprints in the Heart

Your footprints are still in my heart,
engraved like indelible signs,
every step we took together,
every moment shared,
is a memory I carry with me.

Even as time passes,
your footprints do not fade,
they remain there,
reminding me how deep our bond was.

Every day, I sit and think of you,
how you filled my life with joy,
with unconditional love,
with a presence that asked for nothing
but to be loved.

Your footprints are a map,
that guides me through memories,
a path of love and sweetness,
that always brings me back to you.

Even though I can no longer see you,
I feel your presence,
in the footprints you left,
in the heart that still beats for you.

A Distant Hug

Your embrace is a distant memory,
but I still feel it,
like a warmth that never fades,
that envelops me in the coldest nights.

Even though you are no longer here,
the memory of your love comforts me,
keeps me company,
in every moment of solitude.

Your hug lives in me,
a memory that never fades.

The Sweetness of Memory

Every memory of you is sweet,
like honey on my lips,
a taste I will never forget,
that I will carry with me forever.

Even on the bitterest days,
the sweetness of your memory
fills me with comfort,
reminds me how lucky I was.

A Song of Memory

Your memory is a song of memory,
a melody that resonates in my heart,
each note is a fragment of us,
of what we shared.

Even though I can't hear your voice anymore,
the song still plays,
it takes me back in time,
to those days of pure happiness.

Every time the world is silent,
I hear that song in my heart,
a symphony of memories,
that binds me to you forever.

A Story to Tell

Your memory is a story to tell,
a tale I carry in my heart,
made of special moments,
of days I will never forget.

Every time I close my eyes,
I relive our story,
every detail, every smile,
is a chapter that I reread with love.

Even if you are no longer here,
the story is not over,
it continues to live in me,
in the words I never stop speaking.

I tell anyone who will listen about you,
how much you loved me,
how much you taught me,
how you changed my life.

Your story is imprinted in my heart,
a tale that knows no end,
and that I will continue to tell,
until my last breath.

A Whisper in the Night

The night brings with it the memory of you,
a whisper that speaks to me sweetly,
tells me about you, about how you were,
about how you still are in me.

Even when the darkness is total,
your whisper lights up my heart,
reminds me that I am not alone,
that your love still lives.

Lights of Memory

Your memories are lights in my mind,
shining in the darkest moments,
each light is a fragment of us,
a piece of the past that never fades.

Even when all seems lost,
the lights of memory guide me,
bring me back to you,
to the warmth of your embrace.

These lights illuminate my path,
they remind me that you never went away.

The Wind of the Past

The wind of the past carries with it your memory,
a breath that touches my skin,
takes me back in time,
to when we were together.

Every breeze speaks to me of you,
of those happy and carefree days,
of a love that knew no end,
and that still lives in me.

Even though time has separated us,
the wind does not forget,
it carries with it your scent,
a memory that never fades.

A Memory of Sweet Moments

Every memory of you is sweet,
a moment I cherish,
a precious gem in my heart
that shines even on the darkest of days.

I think back to those moments spent together,
with a smile and a tear,
because even if you are no longer here,
your memory still warms me.

Sweet moments that I will never forget,
and that I will carry with me, always.

Reflections of the Heart

My heart reflects on what we shared,
every moment, every caress,
is a reflection of love,
a thought that brings me back to you.

I think back to how you looked at me,
with those eyes full of affection,
how you were always there,
ready to give me your love.

Even now, when the world grows dark,
the reflections of my heart
bring me back to your sweetness,
to your infinite patience.

Every reflection is a journey into the past,
a return to those happy days,
which are now only memories,
but which still live in me.

My heart reflects,
and in every reflection,
I find a piece of you,
a love that never fades.

A Light That Never Goes Out

Your memory is a light that never goes out,
it shines in my heart every day,
it guides me in difficult moments,
it reminds me how special you were.

Even though you are no longer here,
your light continues to shine,
a beacon that guides me
in the stormy sea of life.

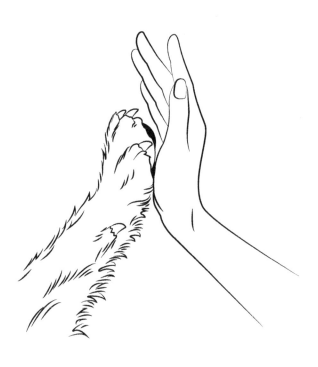

"We should not cry because he left us, but smile because he gave us his love."
Gabriel García Márquez

THE HEALING

Petals in the Wind

Like petals in the wind,
memories fly lightly,
carrying with them the pain,
transforming it into sweet nostalgia.

Each petal is a fragment of you,
which dissolves into the air,
leaving a scent of peace,
which heals the wounds of the heart.

Towards the Light

In the darkness of grief,
I found a distant light,
a glimmer that guided me
toward a new beginning.

Every step towards the light
has brought me closer to you,
not in physical presence,
but in a luminous memory.

Now I walk towards the light,
carrying your love with me.

A New Dawn

After the long night of pain,
a new dawn has risen,
bringing with it the hope
of brighter days.

The sun dried my tears,
and with every ray,
it warmed my heart,
giving me the strength to move forward.

Your memory has become my guide,
a beacon in the storms of life,
and in this new dawn,
I have found the peace I was looking for.

Scars of Love

Scars on the heart
are not signs of weakness,
but testimonies of love,
of a bond that cannot be broken.

Every scar tells a story,
of pain and healing,
of how love, even after loss,
continues to live, to flourish.

Time That Heals

Time, like a skilled sculptor,
has shaped my pain,
transforming it into a form of beauty,
which I now carry in my heart.

It didn't erase your memory,
but it made it sweeter,
a peaceful thought
that accompanies me every day.

Time has healed the wounds,
leaving room for peace.

A Breath of Serenity

After the storm,
I found a breath of serenity,
a moment of quiet,
where your memory enveloped me.

No longer as a shadow of pain,
but as a light caress,
which reminded me of the love
we shared,
and which continues to live in me.

In that breath, I found peace,
a serenity that filled my soul,
and I understood that, despite the loss,
your love will always be my strength.

Bloom Again

The pain has dug deep furrows,
but it is precisely in those furrows
that healing has begun to blossom,
like flowers that grow from arid earth.

Every tear was a seed,
every memory was nourishment,
and over time,
a garden of peace came to life in my heart.

I have learned to bloom again,
to find beauty in the scars,
to see your love in every flower,
in every new dawn.

Even though your physical presence is missing,
your spirit lives on in this garden,
a place of serenity and hope,
where I can take refuge
whenever the pain returns.

And so, I bloom again,
carrying with me your memory,
which accompanies me,
in every season of my life.

Finding the Strength Again

When I thought I couldn't do it,
your memory gave me strength,
lifted me from the abyss,
bringing me towards the light.

I have found the strength to live,
to smile and to love again,
because I know that you are always with me,
in the beat of my heart.

A Sea of Peace

The sea of pain was deep,
but I learned to swim,
to let myself be lulled by the waves,
until I reached a shore of peace.

Each wave brought with it a memory,
but also a promise of healing,
and now, on the shore of serenity,
I find comfort in your love.

The sea has calmed,
and with it, my heart.

Healing Cycles

Healing is a continuous cycle,
an alternation of pain and peace,
of bright days and fleeting shadows,
which eventually lead to a new dawn.

I have learned to accept every stage,
to not fear the dark days,
because I know that even after the longest night,
the sun will shine again.

Each cycle brings me closer to you,
not as a ghost from the past,
but as a reassuring presence,
accompanying me on the journey of life.

A Caress in the Wind

In the wind I feel a caress,
a light touch on my face,
that reminds me of your love,
and fills me with a sweet peace.

Even though you are no longer here,
the wind carries your spirit with it,
a caress that comforts me,
and helps me heal.

The Path of Healing

I walk along the path of healing,
with slow but sure steps,
every stone a reminder of you,
every curve a challenge overcome.

The pain has become a companion,
but it no longer scares me,
because I know that at the end of this path,
I will find the peace I seek.

And along the way, I feel your presence,
guiding and protecting me.

The Heart is Reborn

From the ashes of pain,
my heart is reborn,
like a phoenix rising,
stronger and wiser than before.

Every tear has watered the ground,
where memories now bloom,
no longer as painful thorns,
but as flowers of peace and love.

The heart is reborn with new strength,
ready to face life,
carrying with it your memory,
like a light that never goes out.

Waves of Healing

The waves of the sea speak to me of healing,
with their slow and constant movement,
they remind me that pain comes and goes,
but in the end it subsides,
leaving room for peace.

Every wave is a thought of you,
crashing gently on the shore,
taking away a little of my pain,
and leaving behind a sense of calm.

I have learned to let go,
to not hold back the tears,
because I know that each wave of healing
brings me closer to serenity.

The sea teaches me to live in the present,
not to fear the future,
because even when the waves rise,
I know that I can count on your love,
which supports me, which guides me,
through every storm,
until I reach the shore,
where healing awaits me.

A Ray of Hope

In the darkness of pain,
I saw a ray of hope,
a light that illuminated my path,
guiding me towards healing.

That ray was your memory,
a thought that lifted me up,
and rekindled in me the desire to live,
to find peace again.

Rebirth

From the rubble of pain,
a new life was born,
a slow and sweet rebirth,
which led me to rediscover serenity.

Every day is a step forward,
towards a brighter future,
where your memory is no longer a burden,
but a source of strength and love.

Rebirth is a precious gift,
which I welcome with gratitude.

The Inner Light

Deep in my heart,
I found a hidden light,
a flame that never goes out,
even in the deepest darkness.

This light is your love,
which continues to shine within me,
guiding me towards peace,
illuminating the path of healing.

The Awakening of the Heart

Like a flower blooming in the sun,
my heart slowly awakens,
after the long winter of pain,
welcoming the sweetness of memories.

Every day is a new spring,
where pain turns into strength,
and the memory of you becomes a comfort,
a balm for the wounds of the soul.

The heart awakens to life,
ready to beat again, with serenity.

Rainbow of Hope

After the incessant rain,
a rainbow appears on the horizon,
bringing with it the colors of hope,
a promise of brighter days.

The pain dissolves like fog,
making room for light,
and in the colors that illuminate the sky,
I see your eternal love reflected.

Every shade is a memory,
every ray a new possibility,
to live with a light heart,
carrying your essence with me, always.

Beyond the Clouds

Above the dark clouds of sorrow,
the sky is always clear,
and even when my heart is heavy,
I know that peace is there, waiting for me.

Beyond the tears, beyond the sadness,
there is a place of serenity,
where the memory of you does not hurt,
but brings only sweetness and comfort.

The journey is long, the road is winding,
but every step brings me closer to the light,
every breath is a step towards healing,
a return to inner peace.

And when the sun shines again,
it will be a new beginning,
a day when the pain will be just a shadow,
and your memory a light that never goes out.

"An animal we have loved
never really goes away. It
walks beside us day after
day, invisible, silent, but
always near, still loved, still
lost."
Anonymous

THE SPIRITUALITY

Free Souls

Now you are a free soul,
flying beyond the stars,
no longer tied to the earth,
but part of the infinite.

I feel you in the blowing wind,
in every ray of sunshine,
you are everywhere and nowhere,
always with me, in my heart.

Light Among the Stars

Looking up at the night sky,
I see a star shining brighter,
I know it's you, watching over me,
a beacon of light in the darkness.

Every star tells a story,
and yours shines with eternal love,
reminding me that you are not far away,
but always near, in a peaceful place.

You have become part of the universe,
a light among the stars that never goes out.

Beyond the Rainbow Bridge

It is said that beyond the Rainbow Bridge,
there is a place of peace and joy,
where the spirits of animals
find rest and eternal happiness.

I imagine you, running free,
no more pain or worry,
bathed in a golden light,
surrounded by love and serenity.

I know that one day we will meet again,
beyond that bright bridge,
where time no longer exists,
and love is the only law.

A Guardian Angel

I like to think that you are now an angel,
a guardian watching over me,
guiding me in dark times,
protecting me with your light.

Even though I can't see you,
 feel your presence next to me,
a love that doesn't fade,
but grows in another dimension.

In the Morning Wind

In the morning wind,
I feel your spirit near,
a light breath that touches me,
a memory of a love that never dies.

Every dawn brings with it your greeting,
a message of peace and serenity,
it reminds me that you are always here,
an energy that lives in eternity.

You are the wind that gently embraces me,
a whisper that guides me through life.

The Embrace of Infinity

When the sky turns red,
and day gives way to night,
I feel the embrace of infinity,
which envelops me with your love.

You have become part of something bigger,
a presence that transcends time,
a love that knows no bounds,
that lives in every star and every breath.

Even though I can no longer see you,
I know you are always with me,
in the air I breathe,
in the energy that surrounds me.

An Eternal Bond

Our bond has not broken,
it has simply transformed
into an invisible thread that unites us,
from this life to eternity.

Even though the earthly world has let you go,
your spirit remains with me,
a silent guide in my steps,
a love that knows no death.

I walk with you beside me,
even if I can't see you,
I feel your warmth,
your constant and reassuring presence.

Time cannot erase what is eternal,
and our love lives beyond the stars,
in a place where there are no goodbyes,
only encounters that last forever.

It comforts me to know that you are free,
part of the infinite,
a soul that watches over me,
until the day we meet again.

In the Light of Sunset

As the sun sets,
I see your face in the sunset light,
a reflection of peace and serenity,
a sign that reminds me of your presence.

Every sunset is a greeting,
a moment of spiritual connection,
where I feel your eternal love,
illuminating my life.

A Divine Whisper

Your spirit speaks to me in silence,
a divine whisper that reassures me,
tells me that you are at peace,
in a place where love is eternal.

Every time I close my eyes,
I hear your voice guiding me,
comforting me and giving me hope,
in a world that seems brighter.

You are the whisper that brings serenity,
a divine presence
that never abandons me.

The Circle of Life

The circle of life does not break,
it continues to turn, endlessly,
and I know that you too are part of this cycle,
a soul that lives beyond time.

You have left this earth,
but your spirit remains,
in every thing I touch,
in every breath I take.

The circle will reunite us one day,
in a place where there are no goodbyes,
only an eternal love,
that binds us forever.

In the Quiet of the Morning

In the silence of the morning,
I feel your presence near,
a calm that envelops me,
a memory of peace and love.

Each new day is a gift,
a sign that your spirit lives on,
guiding me gently,
toward the serenity you have found.

A Spiritual Refuge

Deep in my heart,
I have found a spiritual refuge,
a place where your spirit lives,
and gives me strength every day.

When the world gets tough,
I take refuge in this sacred space,
where your love envelops me,
filling me with peace and serenity.

Your spirit is my refuge,
a place of healing and light.

Beyond the Doors of Time

Beyond the doors of time,
I know you are there,
in a place where there are no borders,
where love reigns supreme.

Doors open in dreams,
where I can hear your voice,
see your smile,
and know you are at peace.

Even though time separates us,
our bond remains strong,
a thread that runs through eternity,
a love that lives beyond every barrier.

The Breath of the Soul

I feel your breath in the air,
an invisible but strong presence,
that envelops me at every moment,
reminding me that I am never alone.

Your spirit lives in the wind,
in the sun's rays that warm me,
in the stars that shine in the sky,
a soul that knows no end.

You speak to me through the silence,
you guide me with your light,
and every day I find comfort,
in knowing that you are always with me.

Your breath is the strength that lifts me,
the love that sustains me,
a bond that no death can break,
because the soul lives beyond the body.

You are part of something bigger,
a breath of the universe,
that accompanies me in every step,
until we meet again.

The Dance of Souls

In every movement of the wind,
I see the dance of souls,
a ballet of light and love,
where you are the protagonist.

Your soul dances free,
in a world made of peace,
and every time the wind blows,
I feel your love embrace me.

Dancing together into eternity,
our souls never separate.

A Bridge of Light

Between this world and the next,
there is a bridge of light,
where souls meet,
and find peace and serenity.

I imagine you, crossing that bridge,
to a place of eternal love,
where there is no more suffering,
only joy and freedom.

Every time I look up at the sky,
 see that bridge shining,
and I know you're there, waiting,
until we meet again.

In the Silence of the Stars

On the quietest nights,
I look at the stars and search for you,
in their silence I find your presence,
a love that shines in eternity.

The stars tell your story,
a journey towards infinity,
where your spirit lives,
free and serene, among the lights of the sky.

Beyond the Veil of the World

Beyond the veil of this world,
I know there is another realm,
where souls find rest,
and live in eternal peace.

Your spirit has found that place,
where there is no pain,
only pure and unconditional love,
a safe haven for eternity.

Beyond the veil, I know you are happy,
and that gives me peace and serenity.

An Invisible Presence

Even though I can no longer see you,
I feel your presence every day,
an energy that surrounds me,
a love that guides me.

You have become part of everything,
of the earth, of the sky, of the air,
a force that does not vanish,
but grows in the invisible.

Every time the wind blows,
I know it's you speaking to me,
a message of hope and peace,
a presence that never leaves me.

The Call of Eternity

The call of eternity is sweet,
a melody that comforts me,
knowing that you are in a place of peace,
gives me strength to face each day.

I imagine you, free and serene,
in a world where love is pure,
where there are no more goodbyes,
only hugs that last forever.

Eternity has separated us physically,
but your spirit remains with me,
a bond that time cannot break,
a connection that goes beyond life.

When I close my eyes, I feel you near,
a whisper of love that guides me,
and I know that eternity is not a goodbye,
but a new beginning,
where we will meet again one day,
to continue our journey together,
beyond the boundaries of time,
in the infinite embrace of eternity.

CONCLUSION

As we come to the end of this journey through the emotions of grief, memory, and healing, it is important to reflect on what we have learned and how we can continue to honor the bond we have had with our animal friends.

The words in this book are a tribute to those special beings who have touched our lives in unique and unforgettable ways.

Even though we can no longer hold them in our arms, their spirits live on in our hearts and memories.

The pain of loss is a sign of the love we have felt, a love that knows no bounds.

This love, which has bound us to our four-legged friends, is eternal.

Though time may dull the sharp pain, the memory of them will remain with us forever, a sweet reminder of what it means to be truly loved.

The lessons we learned from them—faithfulness, the simple joy of small things, living in the moment—are treasures we will carry with us for the rest of our lives.

Now, as you close this book, I invite you to remember the happy moments you have shared with your animal friend.

Think of those moments not as something lost, but as a gift you have received, a gift that will live on within you.

The animals we have loved never truly go away; they live on in our hearts, in our dreams, in the laughter we share when we remember their funny habits, and in the smiles that light up our faces when we think of how much they have given us.

This book is intended to be a virtual hug for all those who are going through the pain of mourning.

You are not alone on this journey, and you have never been alone.

Every poem, every word written here is a sign of solidarity, an invitation to find comfort in the memories and remembrance of the special bond you shared with your animal friend.

Remember, love never dies.

It continues to live through us, transforming itself into memory, into strength, and into gratitude.

May this book be a beacon of hope for you, a companion in your healing process, and a tribute to the wonderful journey you have shared with your four-legged friend.

Thank you for sharing this journey with me.

May the memory of your animal friends always bring you comfort and may their spirits continue to watch over you, wherever you go.

THANKS

Writing this book has been an emotional and intense journey, made possible by the support and love of many people to whom I am deeply grateful.

First of all, I would like to thank everyone who has shared with me their stories of love and loss regarding their animal friends.

Your experiences have inspired me deeply and helped shape this book.

Your sincerity and courage in sharing your pain and joy have been a beacon of light in this project.

A special thanks goes to my family and friends, who have always believed in me and in the value of this book.

Thank you for your unconditional love, your patience and for being my support in the most difficult moments.

Without you, this book would never have become a reality

Finally, my deepest thanks go to my four-legged friends, past and present.
To you, who have filled my life with love, joy, and silent understanding.

This book is dedicated to you and to all the animals who have touched the hearts of their human companions.

Thank you for teaching me what it means to love unconditionally.

To all the readers who have decided to take this journey with me: thank you.

I hope this book can provide comfort, inspiration, and a lasting reminder of the love you shared with your pets.

With all my heart, Rubina Moon

HELP ME IMPROVE, LEAVE ME A REVIEW

Made in the USA
Las Vegas, NV
01 May 2025

21600139R00066